DANGER
THE DOG YARD CAT

To Brooke—
MUSH ON!
June 2010

LIBBY RIDDLES • IDITAROD WINNER
with SHELLEY GILL   Illustrated by SHANNON CARTWRIGHT

DANGER
THE DOG YARD CAT

Manufactured in China in January 2010 by C&C Offset Printing Co. Ltd.
Shenzhen, Guangdong Province

Library of Congress Card Number 89-62186
ISBN 0-934007-20-9 (pbk)
ISBN 0-934007-09-8 (hc)

PAWS IV
Published by Sasquatch Books
119 South Main Street, Suite 400
Seattle, Washington 98104
(206) 467-4300
(800) 775-0817 (book orders)
www.SasquatchBooks.com
Custserv@SasquatchBooks.com

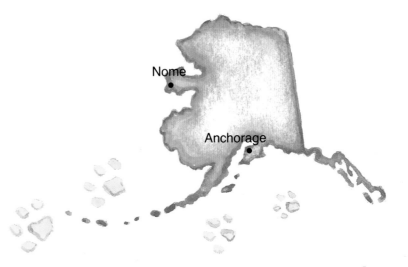

Nome

Anchorage

Dedicated to children who love adventure
You can fly a fast plane or go to the moon.
Climb Mt. Everest or write a slick tune.
Search for lost treasure with a secret gold key.
Hey, you can be anything you want to be.

There once was a cat
of questionable background,
who had done hard time
in the Nome dog pound.

Danger was a cool cat,
some say a fool cat,
a mean, lean
break-all-the-rules cat.

The woman who saved him
was a sled dog racer.
She introduced 57 huskies
to the cool mouse-chaser.

But even our hero
was taken aback,
to see his new partners
chewing the fat.

So here is his story
and here is the tale.
How Danger the cat,
had to pay for his bail.

Up this far north
where life is tough,
it's hard to find a cat
who's got the right stuff.

You can freeze off your whiskers
when the north wind blows.
Walk around barefoot
you'll freeze all your toes.

Hitching rides in a dog sled
can leave you exposed.
Peek out of the sled bag
you frostbite your nose.

It's no piece of cheese,
the life that I lead...
all these dang dogs
always chase after me.

The pups are the worst
when they get to run free.
They get lots of kicks
out of bothering me.

First Fidget, then Meatloaf
will join in the fun.
A poor hardworking cat
can't even laze in the sun.

But Mudshark's my buddy,
he's cross-eyed and lean.
Forty-five pounds
of sled pulling machine.

Come midnight when I'm lying
all snug in my bed,
visions of sled dogs
race round in my head.

On those nights I dream
I'm a sabre-toothed cat,
back in the days when
they had things like that.

If I had those fangs
I'd get some respect.
Those pups would see me coming
and they'd all run like heck.

You would think in the winter
it would be nice and quiet,
but when those dogs get hitched up
it starts a small riot.

In March the team's excited.
All tense about the race,
bragging that they'll run and run
until they're in first place.

But here comes the boss
with a worried face;
seems she's minus a good leader
and can't run in the big race.

The team is howling,
shivering and crying.
Their big day is over
without even trying.

Then my buddy Mudshark
barks out a plan.
Next thing I know
I'm part of their clan.

START

They're lined up behind me.
Hey, how about that?
For the first time in history
the lead dog is a cat!

Now we're off the starting line-
there goes the gun!
They're all running to catch me
but here comes the fun-

No matter how fast
these furry pups go,
I'm in lead cat position:
They're just dust in the snow.

It's just like at home
when they track me and chase me.
But on this run to Nome
they'll never outrace me!

On through the mountains
over the sea
they strain and they struggle
but they can't catch me.

We're at the finish line,
first team in!
At the cameras I flash my best
tough-guy cat grin.

The Nome Nugget
Alaska's Oldest Newspaper
DANGER

They feed me a dinner
of mousies and shrews...
a feast fit for a winner,
a cat who makes news.

Now that we're home
things'll be different. You'll see.
The sled dogs of Nome
will all bow down to me.

They'll say:
There goes that cool cat
that break-all-the-rules cat
that dangerous lead cat.
Yeah, there goes Danger.

THE END

Danger at home in Nome.

DANGER THE DOG YARD CAT

Talkin Blues

There's 57 dogs that aren't the same
Some are fancy and some are plain
And some are wild and some are tame
And each one's got a different name

There's Dugan and Axle and Handsome Sam
Basil and Blondie and Steely Dan
Inca, Speedy and Judy Blue
Prince Mutt, Miles and Pirate too.
Isiah Thomas and Magic J
Worthy, McHale and Lady Day
And Don't forget Pal and Wags and Slipper
Fat Miss Minnow and her sister Tipper
There's Indy, Ida, Sushi and Black,
Binga, Bugsquito barkin' out back
Flounder, Sockeye, Grayling and Trout
Good Ole Mudshark with his pointy snout
There's Motor Mouth, Tiny, Girla and Bane
Specs and Fast and just the same
Grantly, Nova, Whoopi and Sting
Ajax, Muchacha, Herc thinks he's King.
But of all the dogs around this place
The cat's the one who saved the race
So gather 'round if you wanna hear
The story of Danger and his career.
What a career.

Frozen Cat Paw Blues

Right paw, left paw, front paw, rear
Pick 'em up quick or you're going to hear
The whining cat call of a fellow whose
Got a case of the frozen cat paw blues

I wish I had those husky pads
Then old Mudshark would think I'm bad
I'd settle for a nice warm pair of shoes
I gotta pick 'em up quick or get the
frozen cat paw blues

Everyday it's the same
Keep on moving or face the pain
My shiny claws I don't want to lose
To those frozen cat paw blues

I'm Not a House Cat (With the Cat Scats)

Ah kitty no use to look for me
I won't be where I should be
I won't be a laying inside
I'll be out on a sled takin' a ride

I'm not spouse cat
House cat
Mouse cat
I'm a lead cat,
Speed cat,
Freed cat

Don't expect me to purr and play
I'm used to doing things my own way

This cool cat is on the go
When there's lots of ice and snow
If it reads forty below
Well that just is magnifico.

It's A Dog's Life

Well it's a dog's life for this old cat
Up in the Arctic is where I'm at
Fightin' with the Huskies
Holdin' my own
Sinkin' my teeth into a big moose bone
Well I ain't that smart
But I can see
You can be anything you wanna be.
Though it might sound strange
I know that
It's a dog's life for this old cat.

Danger

She's up in the morn
She's ready to go
She's just been warned
It's starting to snow

Gonna be a storm
A bad one too
But she don't care
Cause she knows what she's gotta do

There ain't no doubt she loves danger
And Danger loves her too.

She's running alone
She's headin' to Nome
She's wondering if she'll ever
   find her way home
But it won't be the last thing
She'll ever do
Because of a secret I'll share with you

There ain't no doubt she loves danger
And Danger loves her too.

Get Up and Go

There's a storm comin' on
And it's movin' fast
This chance just may be our last
If you want to win
You've got to give it all
So it's on your feet dogs and hear my call.

Get up and go, get up and go,
Get up and go, I want to get movin' on.
Get up and go, get up and go,
Get up and go, I wanna get back to Nome.

Well we're almost there and we got the lead
Come on dogs gimme a little more speed
There ain't gonna be no time to rest
So it's on your feet dogs and do your best.

Fish Head Stew

Don't want no food
That comes from a can
And I don't care if it's catfood or spam
Gotta have real food
If I'm going to survive
It's fish head stew that keeps me alive.

Fish head, fish head, fish head stew
Fish heads looking back at you
Makes me feel good through and through
Gotta have some fish head stew.

When I get home
Well I won't be blue 'cause I can have
some fish head stew
and if you'd like
I'll share some with you
Fish head, fish head, fish head stew.

Danger - The dog yard cat
Songs by Hobo Jim and Libby Riddles
Copyright Paws IV Publishing 1989

THE ALASKA ABC BOOK

KIANA'S IDITAROD

MAMMOTH MAGIC

ALASKA MOTHER GOOSE

THUNDERFEET

DANGER – The Dog Yard Cat

ALASKA'S THREE BEARS

NORTH COUNTRY CHRISTMAS

COUNT ALASKA'S COLORS

IDITAROD CURRICULUM

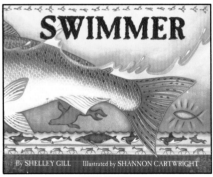

SWIMMER

DENALI CURRICULUM

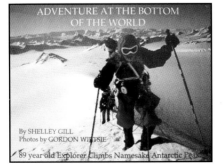

ADVENTURE AT THE BOTTOM OF THE WORLD

STORM RUN

Titles available from PAWS IV

Published by Sasquatch Books
119 South Main Street, Suite 400
Seattle, Washington 98104
(206) 467-4300
(800) 775-0817 (book orders)
www.SasquatchBooks.com
Custserv@SasquatchBooks.com